Sense and Sentiments

Sense and Sentiments

ANITA PHELPS LOCKHART-SPAINHOWER

Sense and Sentiments

Copyright © 2023 by Anita Phelps Lockhart-Spainhower. All rights reserved.

No part of this publication may be reproduced, stored in a retrieval system or transmitted in any way by any means, electronic, mechanical, photocopy, recording or otherwise without the prior permission of the author except as provided by USA copyright law.

The opinions expressed by the author are not necessarily those of URLink Print and Media.

1603 Capitol Ave., Suite 310 Cheyenne, Wyoming USA 82001
1-888-980-6523 | admin@urlinkpublishing.com

URLink Print and Media is committed to excellence in the publishing industry.

Book design copyright © 2023 by URLink Print and Media. All rights reserved.

Published in the United States of America

ISBN 978-1-68486-413-3 (Paperback)
ISBN 978-1-64367-000-3 (Hardback)
ISBN 978-1-68486-414-0 (Digital)

15.03.23

Dedicated to my family, for their help and support, my parents for sharing their outlook on life with me, and several special friends for their encouragement and faith, and to kindred spirits everywhere.

Contents

A Joyous Memory 9
Pro and Con 10
A Special Place 12
Last of an Angry Man 14
Ode to the Season's End 16
A New Venture 17
The Old Stone Barn 18
My Shadow Love 20
Hymn from My Heart 22
Spring.. 23
A Season to Rest 24
Moonlight 25
Mountain Echo 26
Snowy Eve 28
Restful Waters... 29
I Remember 30
My Shady Lady Love 32
Ode to the Odd Pioneers...33
Snowmobiling 34
To Margo 35
My Son Paul 36
Our Son 37
Sierra Blanca... 38
The Right One... 39
Someone to Lean On 40
Mother's Helper...41
Fat Lady's Lament.. 42
Which Witch? 43
Isometrics (For Your Wrist) 44

A Joyous Memory

Remember the glen where we walked that day?
And the stones we skipped across the bay?
That lovely place that stood serene.
I treasure the memory of the scene.

The ripple of water that washed away
Our worries, our problems could not stay.
It stands alone on the roll of time
The thought of it always rests my mind.

Like children we laughed and played with glee.
Forgetting a while that we were not free
To walk this way again and yet
Tho' our paths have parted, I can't forget.

Pro and Con

"What do you have, that we don't?"
Asked the city man, with pride.
As he walked with his farmer cousin
'Round the quiet country side.

"We've trees and great large buildings,
Parks galore the whole town through.
Now you're getting older,
City living should be for you."

Softly spoke the thoughtful farmer,
As he looked around his farm.
"No, I s'pose there's really nothing
There, could do me any harm.

"But I'd miss the clean white winter snow
And the deep green of grass in spring.
Tho' when it comes to mowing it,
I cuss like anything.

"There's fields to walk and woods to search
And there's the pond we stocked with perch.
Tho' fishing time comes very little,
And my walking bones are getting brittle.

"I'm awful glad you city folk
Don't relish this with glee.
For selfishly, I guess it's cause
It leaves more room for me."

A Special Place

Near a quiet peaceful inlet
Down the hill beyond my door,
Lies a haven which awaits me
There my spirits to restore.

In the evening, when I'm weary
And my life seems full of care
I hasten to my secret harbor,
Knowing rest attends me there.

Green the boughs which hover o'er me.
Soft the moss beneath my feet.
Sweet the scents of Mother Nature
These alone make life replete.

Scarlet are my trees in Autumn.
Master Painter, Splendid Art.
Soon the leaves will pave the pathway
Feathered friends will then depart.

White the snows of winter magic,
Coveting the earth laid bare.
Spring will come and then my haven
Blooms again with.tender care.

Gift that love created for thee.
Molded gently, meant to share.
This is home as God intended
Eden can be anywhere.

Last of an Angry Man

At rest now
The end has finally come.
Your master called
Summoning you home.

The saddest thing of all
I note is this.
Nothing ever
Seemed to bring you bliss.

The ingredients were there.
Strong sons, lovely daughters
You wouldn't let them care.

To reap love you must sow it
This I know.
In your garden of friendship
No flower did grow.

You're gone now
And you cannot retort.
But I do not attempt to judge
I just report.

No one can say
You left no mark, there's one.
Your legacy to us is this—
Your angry son.

Ode to the Season's End

Sadly now, the season ends
Forgotten soon the many friends
The budding friendships cease to be
Until next year when we shall ski—
These slopes and scan the runs to see
Where are those who skied with me?

The taverns echo lonely now
The barren slopes are bleak somehow.
And yet this place is full of ghosts.
Skiers who walked here by the hosts
And memories, one hundred score.
Next year we shall create some more.

But oddly somehow like the snow
My heart has thawed a bit I know.
There are other activities for me to pursue
But still my thoughts shall be with you
And all summer long, I'll truly yearn
For next winter and the snow's return.

A New Venture

Like a moth emerging from darkness
Today you spread your wings.
Escape from your confining cocoon.
Fly on to greater things.

The heights you reach are only bound
By the power of your flight.
The only thing to limit you
Is the earthly creature's fright.

So test your strength
Make this your cry.
I cannot fail
For I only TRY.

The Old Stone Barn

A stately frame of stone remains
Amid the bushes of these plains.
An awesome sight, this barn of stone.
It seems quite lonesome, there alone.
Yet some part of the viewer stays
With ghosts of earlier, hopeful days.

There once a dairy baron sought
To build an empire, so he brought
The best of masons, sturdy rock.
Cleared the land, bought finest stock.
His dream has crumbled, fallen down.
The ruins remain, his broken crown.

But a message it imparts—
Unknown dreams within men's hearts
Are stirred by sight of this, his tower.
A monument to hopes that flower.
Unseen desires entombed within
Encased by bonds so strangely thin.

His labor shall not have been in vain
If just one visitor to this lane
Is driven on to vaster tasks
An inspiration, all he asks.
Once inspired, the bonds will bust.
The key is this, "I can, I must."

My Shadow Love

Strong and steady walks my love
Beside me every day.
Unlike my shadow is my love
Night won't drive him away.

Yet like my shadow is my love
As together through the years
We've shared the roads we travel
Paved with joy or slick with tears.

I'll never be without my love
I'll never walk alone.
Tho' miles and months between us lie
And words I do bemoan.

My thoughts are always with him
They daily span the miles
Happy memories linger with me
They often bring me smiles.

A legacy my love has left me
I smile, I laugh, I sing
A love of life and mankind
Tolerance of everything.

This gift my love has given
More than any other treasure.
Life was meant for living
By the Golden Rule to measure.

Love must not be selfish
And be kept within your heart.
Once you share it with another
Then you'll never be apart.

Hymn from My Heart

In my heart, I sing of Heaven
I have seen and felt the power.
Adirondacks, call me hither
Pines and mountains o'er me tower.

I am small, this much is certain
Yet how fortunate am I.
God has shared his bounty with me
Cast a glimpse of what's on high.

There should never be one person
Who has not shared this view
Peace and love and understanding
Flooded me as it will you.

Overwhelming is His Spirit
Coursing thru me as I see,
All the wonders He's created
For us all, not just for me.

So I bid you, do not falter
There is peace and rest for you
Follow me to Nature's haven,
There your troubles bid "adieu,"

Spring

Today the air is full of spring
Tho' there's fresh snow on the ground.
The robins will be on the wing
A new life's to be found.

So let us too like Nature's things
Begin our lives anew.
Find happiness around us
Since there's so much here to do.

What have you done for God today?
What mark goes in your book?
Did you help another on his way?
Give a stranger a pleasant look?

For unless we treat all men the same
As children from above.
They shall not live the Golden Rule
Or seed the world with love.

A Season to Rest

Lord have mercy on turn
The ones I left below.
To ease their pain, let them understand
This fact that they should know.

Tell them if I could not walk
'Mid my forests green and tall
That I prayed to you, I'd rather
Not walk anywhere at all.

They all know how I loved the
Wooded land, Land of my birth.
And as sure as there's a heaven
I had a taste of it on earth

In the blessed holy season
When these lands were white with snow.
It probably seemed real sad to them
That it was then I had to go.

If they only heard the message
From St. Peter at the Gate
As he opened up the pearly doors,
"It's your time to hibernate."

Moonlight

There is a lovely shining light
That bathes us all with Love.
For everyone appears the same
Under God's candlelight from above.

The moon casts her reflection
No one walks in fear.
Your loved one ne'er seemed lovelier
Silver shines each tear.

The landscape seems completely changed
Into multiple lovely scenes.
How could anyone even dare
To dream naught but lovely dreams.

Yes there's a lovely shining light
That bathes us all with love.
Would we always viewed each other
In God's candlelight from above.

Mountain Echo

Many are the words they've written
Poets, authors gone before
Of my mountains and their glory
I cannot hope to add much more.

Yet I am moved to strive to tell you,
Their effect on me is such.
It's as if I were the first
To see, to hear, to breathe and touch.

Here is God's great glorious Chapel
Lakes and trees and mountains high.
Here I stay in heart and spirit
Modern world may pass me by.

Yet I'll sense no loss, no longing.
Akin to those who lingered here.
In the forest with God's creatures
Running rabbit, tawny deer.

Sparkling waters, towering boulders
Tall green pines, alive with scent.
Send your sinners to the forest
Willingly they'll all repent.

Where else can you sense the spirit?
Cleansing air revives your soul
To remain here is so pleasant
This is now my final goal.

Let me never leave my mountains
This shall be my one loud cry
Here among majestic scenery
Let me live and let me die!

Snowy Eve

The evening seemed transformed
By the softly falling snow.
We looked at each other and
Smiled and said "Let's go!"

Hurriedly we donned our coats,
Our boots, our gloves—ran out the door.
Giggling, trying not to wake the kids
For fear they'd ask "What for?"

How indeed can one explain
The need to rush away
To tramp the snow together
At the end of a long tired day.

We need these precious moments
That seem to be so few.
To just enjoy each other
And whisper, "I love you!"

Restful Waters

Softly lapping at the shoreline
Rippling waters at my door.
Glowing sunset in the distance
One could never wish for more.

Quiet forest, green pines waving
Worries leave my wrinkled brow.
Troubles, problems all have left me
No thoughts left, there's only now.

Let the breeze dispel your sorrow
Waft away your smallest care
New strength surges through your body
Faith revives with fresh clean air.

Gentle waters, sing of Heaven
In this quiet country glen.
Man has glimpsed a bit of Eden.
Peace for earth will come again.

I Remember

You're far away
But every day
I still remember.

Your love has died
So has my pride
But I remember.

My love was true
Why am I blue?
Must I remember?

You won't return
Someday I'll learn
Not to remember.

You made me glad
I made you sad
Do you remember?

There's this for me
I'll not be free
If I remember.

The best of all
I do recall
When I remember.

I still have you
My memories too
And I remember.

My Shady Lady Love

I love a tarnished lady
Her shoes soiled with the dirt
Of the byways she has tread
Roads the gentry always skirt.
(Yet I'd walk the same path because she chose it.)

My love has embraced too many men
With compassion her heart is overflowing
She has clasped some to her breast
Unworthy of her knowing.
(But I love her all the more for her charity.)

The quarrelling children around her feet
Are not blue blood and pure.
They do not all share
The same father for sure.
(Still I cherish them for their mother's sake.)

Her heart is good, her virtue is sharing
Her home and her land, her main sin is caring
My love is notorious, her name is well known.
The lady I love is America; my home.

Ode to the Odd Pioneers

The road to the frontier
Is four lanes wide
Where modern-day pioneers
Race side-by-side.

On God's little acre
Is an A-Frame lodge.
And the covered wagon
Is a Chevie or Dodge.

Getting away from it all
Is a worn-out phrase
'Cause outfitting the camper
Is a business that pays.

If you want to be alone
It really is a pity.
'Cause on weekends now, the solitude
Is found downtown in the city.

Snowmobiling

Snowmobiling
It's the new sport of the Kings
And the Smiths and the Joneses too!

Snowmobiling
Makes you feel like you had wings
As you glide cross the snow
'Neath the blue.

Oh the air is so clear
As it zips past your ear.
And the song of the wind
Makes you glow. Oh

Snowmobiling
Is the new sport of the Kings
And the Smiths, and the Joneses too!

To Margo

Why does it seem a family
Cannot be complete
With only just a single child
Even one of the elite?

It seems to me perfection
Is a boy and then a girl.
One you patch their pants
The other's hair you curl.

So our family lacked something
Until you came along.
Now our days are joyous
And our life is full of song.

I know some days we have our spats
But so do all the others.
There is really something special
Between little girls and mothers!

My Son Paul

My son Paul is a good little lad
Tho' there are times when he is quite bad
He leaves a mess with all his toys.
But then don't most little girls and boys?

Sometimes he helps me quite a bit
From chore to chore his hands will flit.
He likes to dust and move things around.
(Sometimes those things are never found!)

He's a sweet little guy, a loving chap
He can talk about this and chat about that.
He gets good grades on his school report,
Tho' his manners sometimes fall real short.

He's his parents' and grandfolks'
Pride and joy.
One thing for sure
He's all real boy.

Our Son

My son is a genius
Of this there's no doubt
Although he's but six
He isn't a lout.

Einstein's theory?
He explained it last night.
Climatic conditions?
He's got those down right.

MY wonderful baby
MY darling boy
MY little angel
MY pride and MY joy!

Last night his Aunt Florence
Came over to eat,
And to see for herself
What she'd heard us repeat.
He giggled, he babbled, He stuck out his tongue
'Til I turned to his father
What's wrong with YOUR son?

Sierra Blanca

The air up here is clear and crisp
The run is firm and dry.
My mountain stretches lazily
Its pine "arms" toward the sky.

I breathe the awesome scenery in.
I hold within my heart.
The memory of the view of this
In case we ever part.

The world up here is not the same
As the crowded towns below,
And often when my way seems hard
In fancy, there, I go.
Shoving off upon the trail
Along the run I glide
With many friends to ski with me—
Free spirits by my side.

This is the place where I belong
My soul shall never roam.
For here it is that I would stay—
My Sierra Blanca home.

The Right One

Every man is the right one
Until the right one comes along.
Every star is a bright one and
Each song is your favorite song.

Every road leads you somewhere
Anywhere, is a good place to be.
But suddenly you discover that
There's only one HE for each SHE.

Someone to Lean On

There is a man I'd like to meet.
For short, I'll call him Bill.
With Bill beside me all the time
My troubles would be nil.

He'd be so very strong and tall
And over me he'd tower.
I'd introduce him formally,
By saying, "Meet WILL POWER."

Mother's Helper

As I lay on my sickbed,
My small son did my chores.
He cleared the table, did the dishes
And even swept the floors.

Cheerfully he made this comment
When performing trash removal.
"What I want for my reward, is the
Good Housekeeping Seal of Approval."

Fat Lady's Lament

If many years ago I'd known
That to lose these pounds, I'd whittle.
When asked "What do you want to be
When you're bigger?" I'd said "Little."

Which Witch?

I watch that witch on television.
HER housework seems so easy.
I've wiggled my nose until it's sore.
It only makes ME sneezy.

Isometrics (For Your Wrist)

I daily get my exercise
When that program's on TV.
As soon as it's on Channel Nine.
I switch to Channel Three.

Recognizing that many poets and authors before her have described her beloved mountains in glowing phrases, she nevertheless expresses her own sentiments, most movingly, that "Their effect on me is such,/ It's as if I were the first/ To see, to hear, to breathe and touch./"

"Here is God's great glorious Chapel," she reverently describes the bucolic beauty of her surroundings of "Lakes and trees and mountains high/ Here I stay in heart and spirit/ Modern world may pass me by." And she questions all city dwellers and such, defiantly, "Where else can you sense the spirit?" She even suggests, "Send your sinners to the forest/ Willingly they'll all repent."

Sinners or no, readers of this cheerful and happy poetry by Anita Lockhart will find their lives ever so much perked up by her happy spirits and sensible joy.

www.ingramcontent.com/pod-product-compliance
Ingram Content Group UK Ltd.
Pitfield, Milton Keynes, MK11 3LW, UK
UKHW022218230426
12048UKWH00016BA/925